8

american popular piano
REPERTOIRE

Compositions by
Christopher Norton

Additional Compositions and Arrangements
Dr. Scott McBride Smith

Editor
Dr. Scott McBride Smith

Associate Editor
Clarke MacIntosh

Book Design & Engraving
Andrew Jones

Cover Design
Wagner Design

A Note about this Book

Pop music styles can be grouped into three broad categories:

■ **lyrical** — pieces with a beautiful singing quality and rich harmonies; usually played at a slow tempo;

■ **rhythmic** — more up-tempo pieces, with energetic, catchy rhythms; these often have a driving left hand part;

■ **ensemble** — works meant to be played with other musicians, or with backing tracks (or both!); this type of piece requires careful listening and shared energy.

American Popular Piano has been deliberately designed to develop skills in all three areas.

You can integrate the cool, motivating pieces in **American Popular Piano** into your piano studies in several ways.

■ pick a piece you like and learn it; when you're done, pick another!

■ choose a piece from each category to develop a complete range of skills in your playing;

■ polish a particular favorite for your local festival or competition. Works from **American Popular Piano** are featured on the lists of required pieces for many festivals and competitions;

■ use the pieces as optional contemporary selections in music examinations;

■ Or…just have fun!

Going hand-in-hand with the repertoire in **American Popular Piano** are the innovative **Etudes Albums** and **Skills Books**, designed to enhance each student's musical experience by building technical and aural skills.

■ **Technical Etudes** in both Classical and Pop Styles are based on musical ideas and technical challenges drawn from the repertoire. Practice these to improve your chops!

■ **Improvisation Etudes** offer an exciting new approach to improvisation that guides students effortlessly into spontaneous creativity. Not only does the user-friendly module structure integrate smoothly into traditional lessons, it opens up a whole new understanding of the repertoire being studied.

■ **Skills Books** help students develop key supporting skills in sight-reading, ear-training and technique; presented in complementary study modules that are both practical and effective.

Use all of the elements of **American Popular Piano** together to incorporate a comprehensive course of study into your everyday routine. The carefully thought-out pacing makes learning almost effortless. Making music and real progress has never been so much fun!

Library and Archives Canada Cataloguing in Publication

Norton, Christopher, 1953-

American popular piano [music] : repertoire / compositions by Christopher Norton ;
additional compositions and arrangements, Scott McBride Smith ;
editor, Scott McBride Smith ; associate editor, Clarke MacIntosh.

To be complete in 11 volumes.
Compact disc inserted on p. [3] of each v. contains instrumental backings for ensemble repertoire and improvisation études.
Publisher's nos.: APP R-00 (level P); APP R-01 (level 1); APP R-02 (level 2); APP R-03 (level 3); APP R-04 (level 4); APP R-05 (level 5).
Contents: Level P -- Level 1 -- Level 2 -- Level 3 -- Level 4 -- Level 5.
Miscellaneous information: The series is organized in 11 levels, from preparatory to level 10, each including a repertoire album, an etudes album, a skills book, a "technic" book, and an instrumental backings compact disc.

ISBN 1-897379-00-5 (level P).--ISBN 1-897379-01-3 (level 1).--ISBN 1-897379-02-1 (level 2).--ISBN 1-897379-03-X (level 3).--
ISBN 1-897379-04-8 (level 4).--ISBN 1-897379-05-6 (level 5).--ISBN 978-1-897379-00-4 (level P).--ISBN 978-1-897379-01-1 (level 1).--
ISBN 978-1-897379-02-8 (level 2).--ISBN 978-1-897379-03-5 (level 3).--ISBN 978-1-897379-04-2 (level 4).--ISBN 978-1-897379-05-9 (level 5).--
ISBN 978-1-897379-06-6 (level 6).--ISBN 978-1-897379-07-3 (level 7).--ISBN 978-1-897379-08-0 (level 8)

1. Piano music--Teaching pieces. I. Smith, Scott McBride II. MacIntosh, S. Clarke, 1959- III. Title. IV. Title: Repertoire

MT222.N883 2006   786.2   C2006-906213-7

LEVEL 8 REPERTOIRE
Table of Contents

Stratford Air

Christopher Norton

Free Bird

Christopher Norton

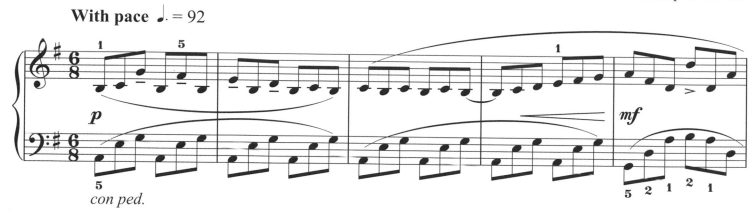

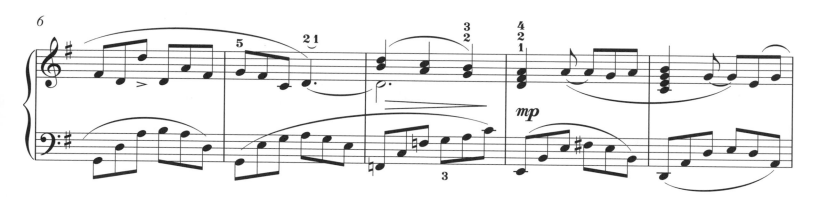

6

Another Thought...

Christopher Norton

Hazy Day

Christopher Norton

Free From Care

Christopher Norton

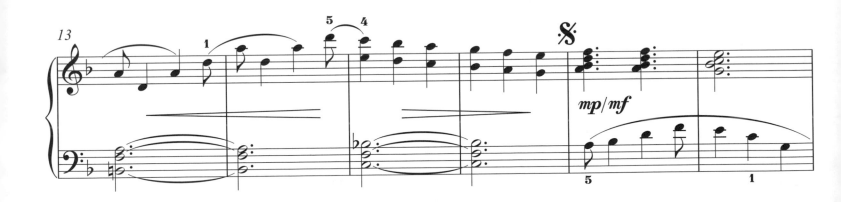

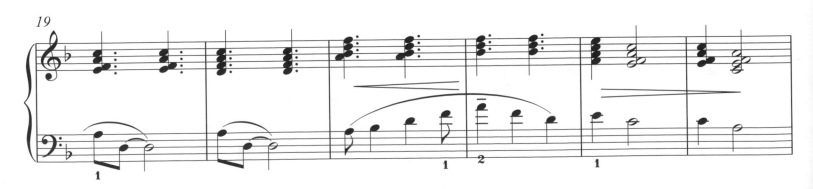

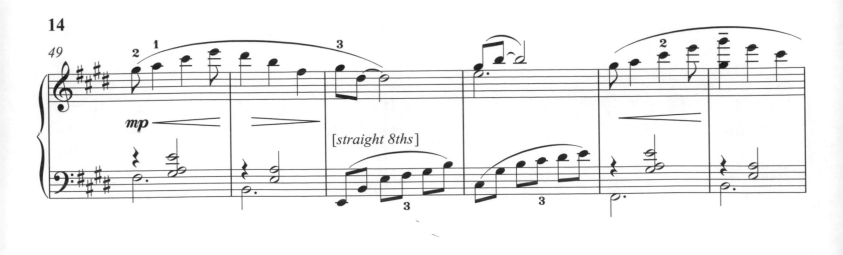

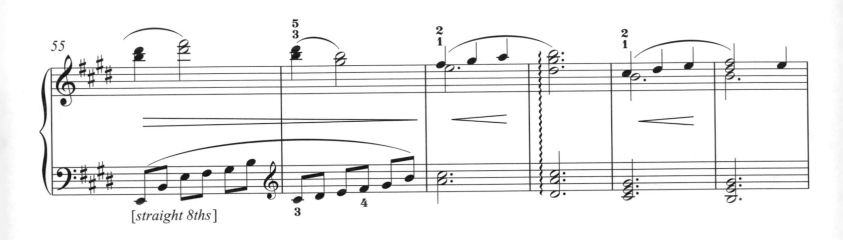

D.S. al coda

The Breakup

Christopher Norton

Song of Farewell

Christopher Norton

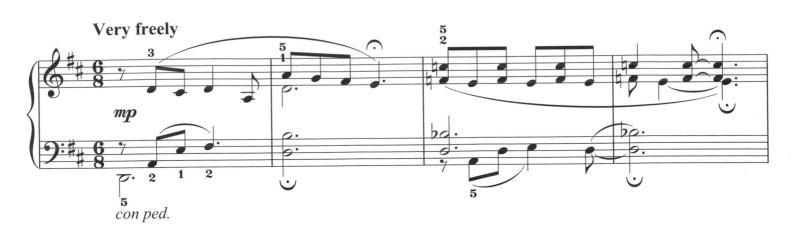

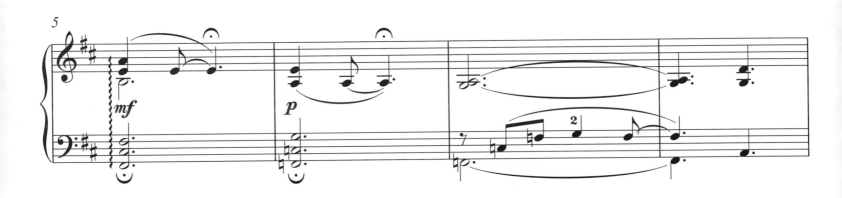

20

Much slower

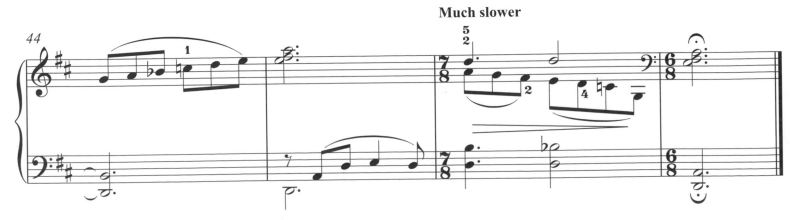

A Night In Lima

Christopher Norton

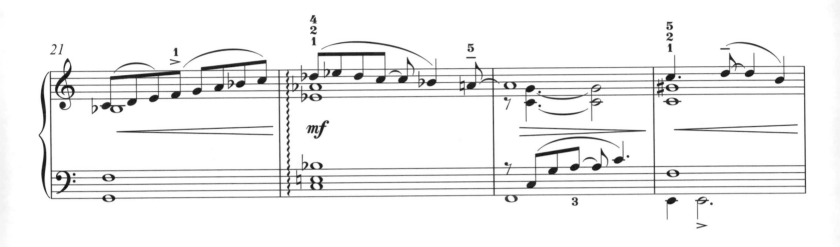

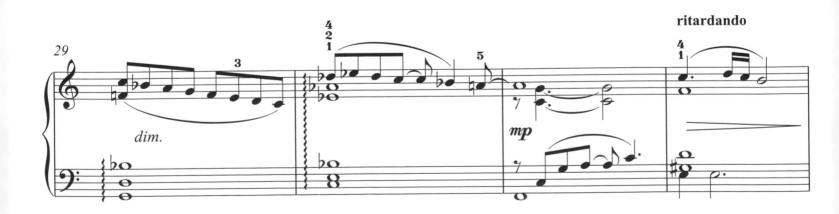

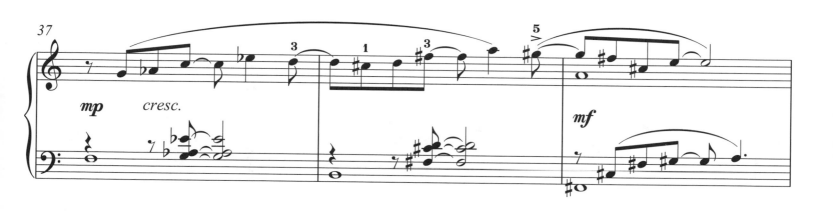

Barbican Blues

Christopher Norton

*) Alternate between the notes as fast as you can.

Red Carpet Day

Christopher Norton

Restless Afternoon

Christopher Norton

Chance Encounter

Christopher Norton

Fingerpickin'

Christopher Norton

Rhythmic ♩ = 126

smoothly

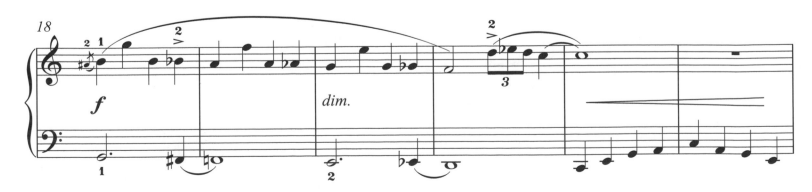

dim.

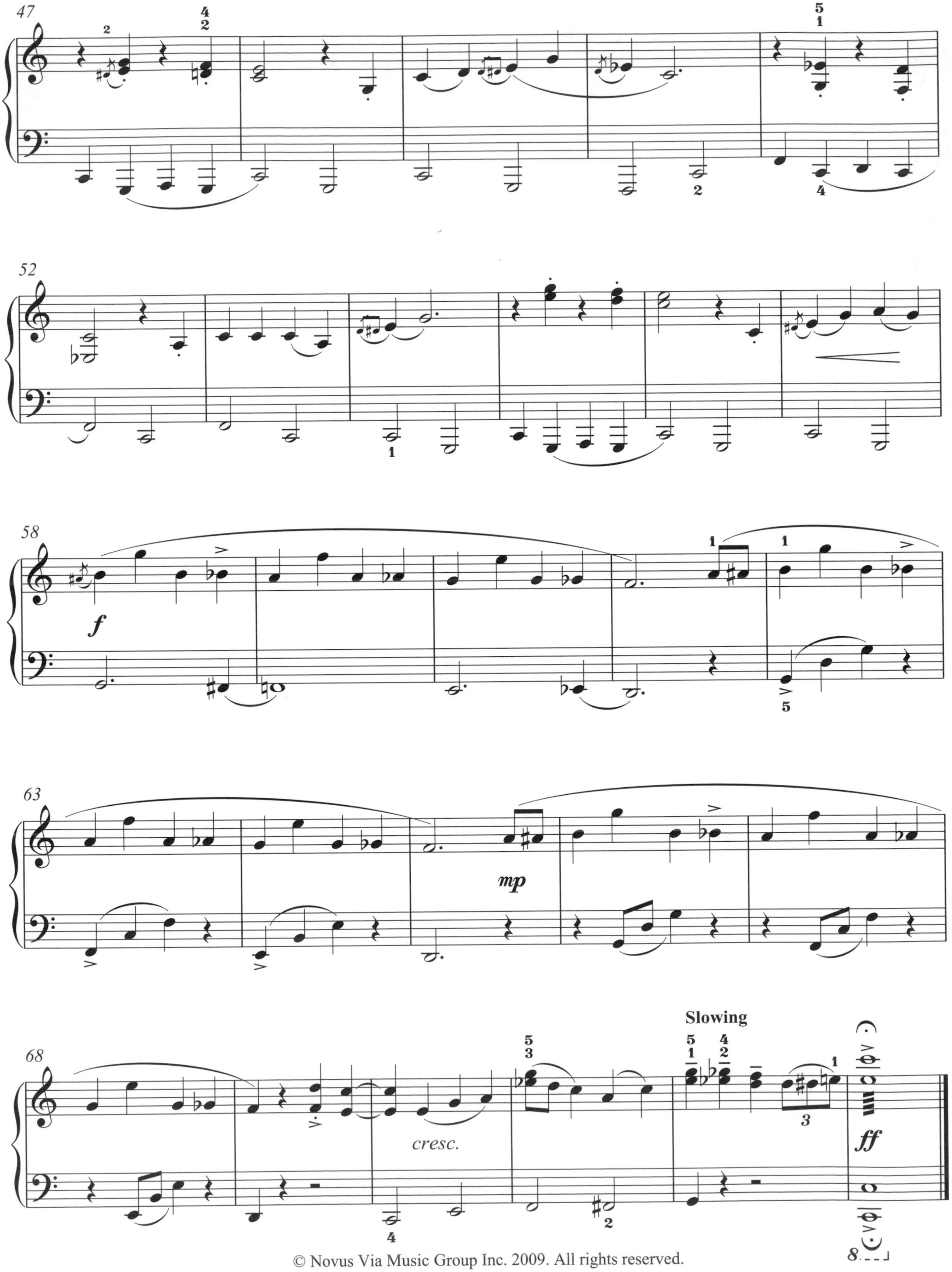
Slowing
cresc.

Crawler

Christopher Norton

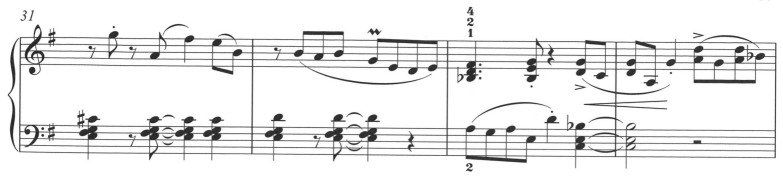

Cosmopolitan

Christopher Norton

Sunny Day

Christopher Norton

44

Sparkling

Christopher Norton

Sparkling

With energy ♩ = 120

Christopher Norton

No Easy Answers

Christopher Norton

Soulful ♩ = 100

No Easy Answers

Christopher Norton

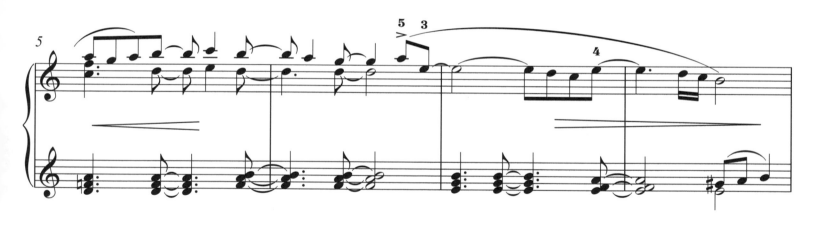

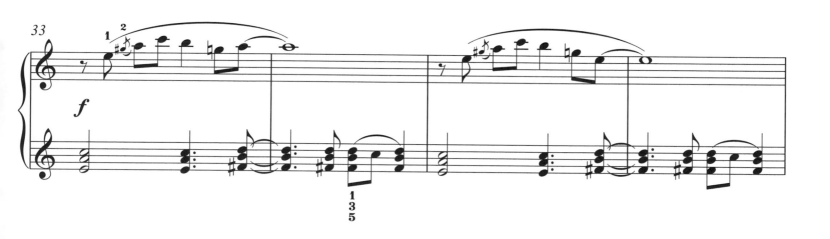

A Day On The Beach

Christopher Norton

Happily ♩ = 132

A Day On The Beach

Christopher Norton

Happily ♩ = 132

FINE

cresc.

D.C. al fine

Unhappy Ending

Christopher Norton

PIANO SOLO

Unhappy Ending

With intensity ♩ = 80

Christopher Norton

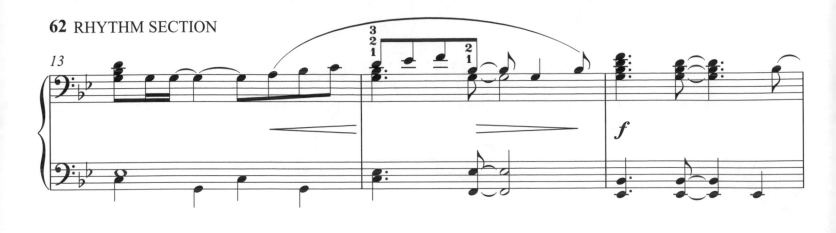

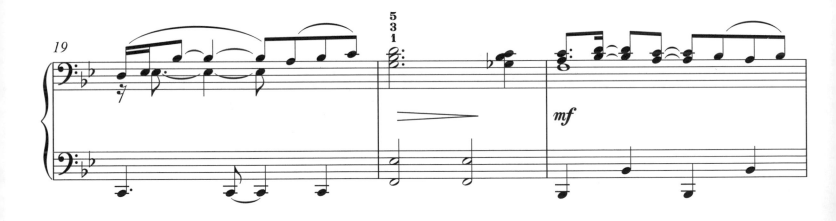

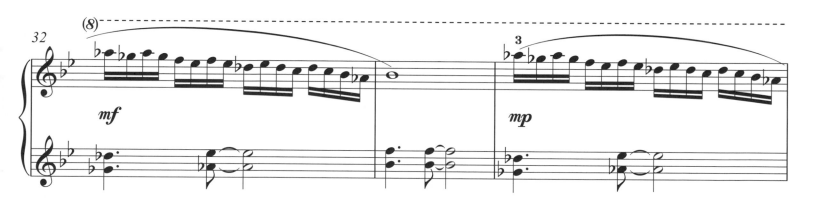

Dawn

Christopher Norton

Dawn

Christopher Norton

Big Blue

Christopher Norton

Big Blue

Christopher Norton

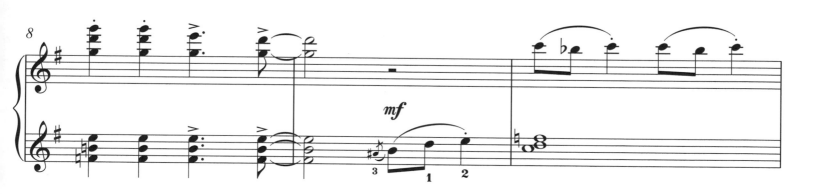

Late At Night

Christopher Norton

Late At Night

Wistfully ♩ = 72

Christopher Norton

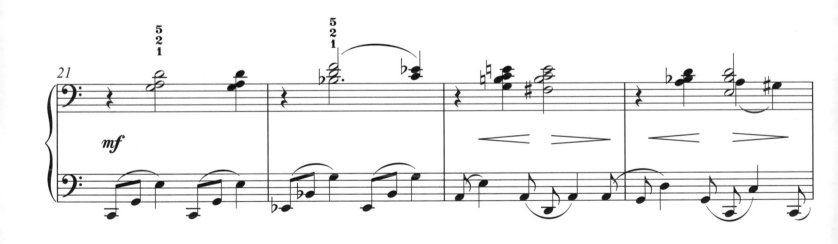

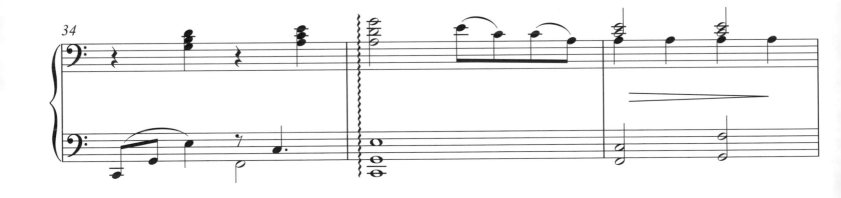

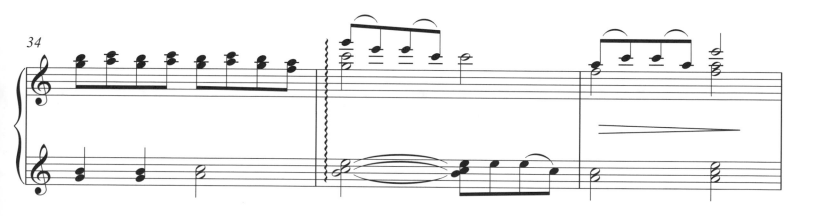

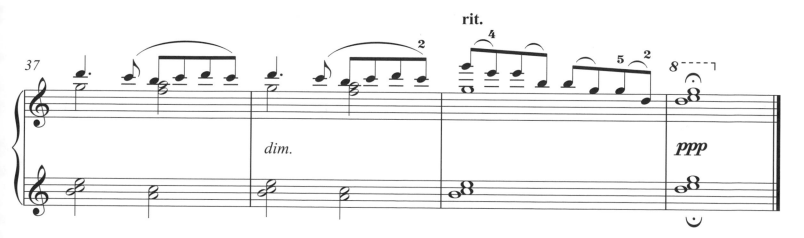

Up and About

Christopher Norton

8 basso sempre

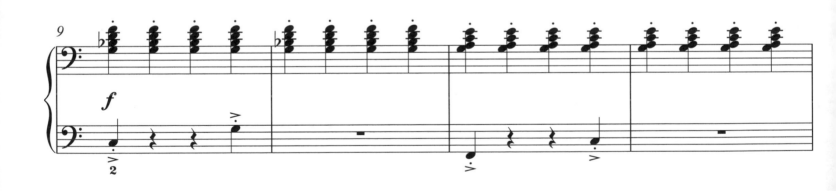

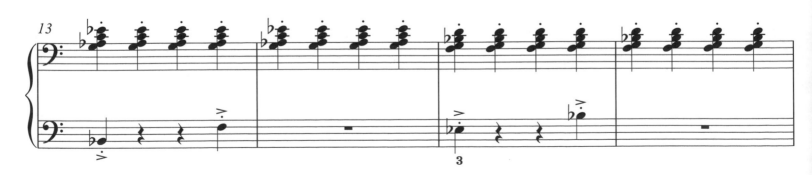

Up and About

Christopher Norton

Very lively ♩ = 132

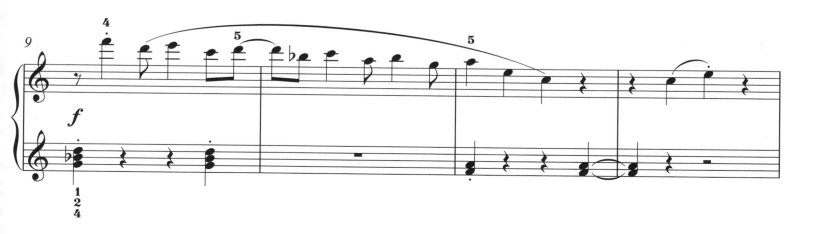

8 basso sempre

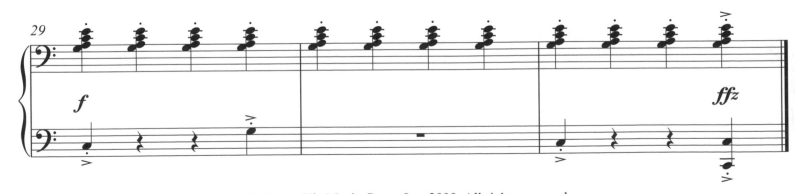

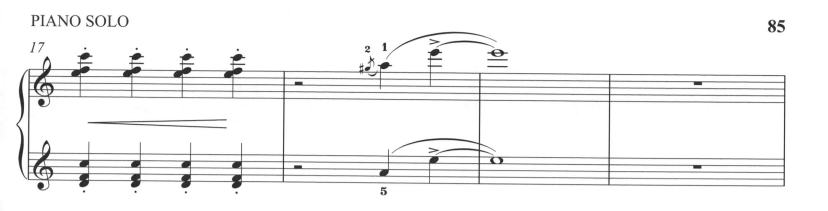

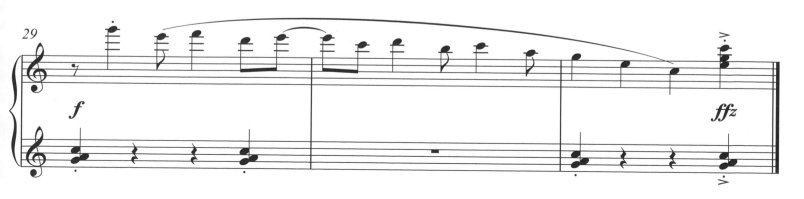

LEVEL 8 REPERTOIRE
Glossary

Backbeat....... The most common rhythm in rock music. There is an emphasis on beats 2 and 4 in a 4-beat bar, usually accented by the drums. Examples include: *A Day at the Beach*

Ballad.......... A slow-tempo popular song. The lyrics are usually concerned with romance, often unhappy. Examples include: *Stratford Air*

Big Band....... A strong rhythm section of piano, upright bass, drums and guitar supporting trumpets, trombones, and saxopones. Popular in the 1940s as an accompaniment to dancing. Examples include: *Red Carpet Day*

Blues........... One of the basic forms of pop music, based on a combination of 19th century African and American song forms. There are many different types. Most feature *blue notes* (notes sung or played below pitch) and often use chords I, IV and V. Examples include: *Big Blue*

Blues shuffle .. A characteristic blues rhythm, based on a loose triplet feel in which the second note of the triplet is left out. There is often a strong bass. Examples include: *Down 'n' Out Blues* (APP 7)

Bolero.......... Refers to several types of Latin dance, usually slow and accompanied by castanets and acoustic guitar. Examples include: *A Night in Lima*

Bossa nova .... A form of Brazilian music, based on the samba, but with more lush, jazz-inflected harmonies. Examples include: *No Easy Answers*

Call and........ A style of singing in which the melodic phrase sung by one singer is "answered" by another. The second phrase often answers a "question" from, or "comments" on the first. Examples include: *Breaking Rocks* (APP 2)

Calypso........ A popular song form from the Caribbean island of Trinidad, using a variety of acoustic guitars and percussion instruments, particularly claves, shaker, and bongos. Examples include: *A Day at the Beach*

Country .... A type of pop ballad with added ballad country elements, especially grace notes. Examples include: *Stratford Air*

Country .... A combination of rock, with rock electric guitars, bass, drums, and a strong backbeat, and country

stylings. Examples include: *Fingerpickin'*

8-beat ballad... A slow to medium tempo sentimental popular song with 8 straight 8th notes per measure. Examples include: *Another Thought*

8-beat rock .... A staple rock 'n' roll rhythmic pattern with 8 eighth notes in every bar, and strong accents on beats 2 and 4. The accents are usually emphasized by the drums. Examples include: *Restless Afternoon, Crawler, Cosmopolitan, Big Blue*

Gospel .... Religious music whose lyrics express spiritual belief. There are several types, often featuring a richly ornamented solo melody, accompanied by full harmonies. Examples include: *Summer Sunday Afternoon* (APP 6)

Jazz .... An American art form, combining African and European elements. The definition of jazz has expanded to include almost all types of popular music. It always features some improvisation.

Jazz ballad..... A short, slow song for piano or with piano accompaniment, often along with bass and drums. It featues rich jazz harmonies. Examples include: *Summer Sunday Afternoon* (APP 6)

Jazz waltz...... A relaxed swing style in 3/4 time. Examples include: *Free From Care*

Latin ballad.... A pop ballad with Latin genre influences. It is often accompanied by acoustic guitar. Examples include: *The Breakup*

Latin 8-beat.... Smooth, medium tempo popular pop songs with Latin rhythms. Examples include: *A Night in Lima, No Easy Answers*

Latin 16-beat .. Uptempo songs with a patern pop of continuous 16th notes, often featuring intricate brass arrangements. Examples include: *Sparkling*

New age .... A peaceful, relaxing musical style, featuring consonant, slow-moving, repetitive chord progressions. Examples include: *Hazy Day*

Pop ballad ..... A slow love song found in nearly all genres of popular music, with many variations. The lyrics usually concern romance. Examples include: *Late at Night*

Pop power ..... Popularised in the 1980s, these ballad medium tempo ballads feature a big drum sound and heartfelt

(some say "over the top") vocals. Examples include: *Unhappy Ending*

Rhumba........ A dance from South America with syncopated right hand chords played over a steady bass part. Examples include: *The Breakup*

Rhythm .... A style of music that combines and blues blues, jazz, and gospel, characterized by strong off-beats and vocal improvisation. Examples include: *Heavy Footed*

Shuffle .... Based on a style of tap dance where the dancer, wearing soft-soled shoes, "shuffles" their feet in a swung 8ths rhythm. Examples include: *Free Bird*

6/8 ballad ..... Gentle, sentimental piano style in 6/8 time. Examples include: *Song of Farewell*

16-beat......... A gentle song style characterized ballad by continuous 16th notes in the accompaniment, often provided by the hi-hat cymbal. Examples include: *Unhappy Ending*

Soul .... An African-American style combining gospel and rhythm and blues.

Stomp.......... A lively, rhythmic style marked by a heavy beat. Its name comes from the "stomping" of the pianist's heel along with the beat. Examples include: *Dingbat Blues* (APP 7)

Stride .... An early jazz piano style featuring the left hand playing 4 beats per measure, with bass notes on beats 1 and 3 and chords two octaves higher on beats 2 and 4. The right hand plays ragtime-influenced syncopated melodies. Examples include: *Barbican Blues*

Swing.......... An uptempo dance style, usually featuring swung 8ths. Examples include: *Barbican Blues*

Swung 8ths .... 8th notes that are notated in equal pairs, but played in a gentle triplet rhythm:

Tango .... A dance originating in Argentina. It is rhythmically strict and often has a snare roll on beat 4.

Walking bass .. A bass style which has quarter notes on every beat, "walking" in scale and chord patterns. Examples include: *Red Carpet Day*

Waltz.......... A dance in 3/4 time, often played with an accent on beat 1. Examples include: *Chance Encounter, Dawn*